THE BRITISH MUSEUM Pocket Timeline of
China

Jessica Harrison-Hall

THE BRITISH MUSEUM PRESS

© 2007 The Trustees of the British Museum

First published in Great Britain by The British Museum Press
A division of The British Museum Company Ltd
38 Russell Square, London WC1B 3QQ
www.britishmuseum.co.uk

ISBN-13: 978-0-7141-3119-1
ISBN-10: 0-7141-3119-9

Jessica Harrison-Hall has asserted the right to be identified as
the author of this work
A catalogue record for this title is available from the British
Library

Designed and typeset in Garamond and Bliss by Turchini Design
Printed in Malaysia

Map on page 31 by Ann Searight and Turchini Design
All photographs are © The Trustees of the British Museum,
courtesy of the Department of Photography and Imaging,
unless otherwise stated: courtesy John Williams: p.4 bottom,
p.15 top and bottom, terracotta warriors in Timeline;
Frances Wood: p.5 top; Gavin Gray: p.5 bottom, p.14 top,
p.26 bottom, p.31 top, Forbidden City and Tian An Men
Square in Timeline; China Cultural Relics Bureau and
Institute of Archaeology, Sichuan Province: p.9 top, bronze
mask from Sanxingdui in Timeline; China Cultural Relics
Bureau and Institute of Archaeology, Beijing: p.9 bottom;
Private collection: p.10 top, jade disc in Timeline; Museum of
the Terracotta Warriors and Horses of Qin Shihuang, Lintong,
Shaanxi Province: p.15 top and bottom, terracotta warriors in
Timeline; National Palace Museum, Taipei: p.26 top;
Wellcome Library, London: acupuncture print in Timeline;
British Library, London (Or.2231, f.51): Empress Wu Zetian
in Timeline.

CONTENTS

INTRODUCTION TO CHINA

Chinese characters can be complex but are beautifully balanced, like this character pronounced 'shou', meaning long life.

CﾟHINA HAS THE WORLD'S longest-surviving great civilization. Chinese people have kept a connection to their past throughout the rise and fall of different dynasties (ruling families). China is home to more than 1.3 billion people, a fifth of the world's population. Today, 92% of these people belong to a single ethnic group. The remaining 8% of the population are from 55 different minorities, each one with its own language and customs.

Chinese is the language spoken by the greatest number of people in the world. Standard Mandarin is the official language. Chinese is the only writing system in the world which has been in continuous use for over two thousand years. Chinese has no alphabet but instead uses characters which can stand for single sounds, whole words or even phrases. More than 40,000 Chinese characters exist. Today you need to know 3,000 characters to read a newspaper.

Spoken Mandarin uses five tones. This means one sound can have five different meanings. 'Ma' can mean mother, hemp, horse, to tell someone off or a question mark, depending on how it is said.

This Chinese woman was photographed reading a newspaper in 2007. You need to know 3,000 different characters to understand the news.

China is a vast country, larger than the whole of Europe, with widely varying climates and landscapes. It is rich in natural resources: coal and gas. In the Gobi Desert in the northwest, temperatures can reach 45° C in the summer. In the northeast, at Harbin, temperatures fall to minus 38° C in winter. China's two greatest rivers are the Huang He (Yellow River) in the north and the Chang Jiang (Yangzi River) in the south. Rice plants grow in flooded fields in the south but wheat and maize are the main crops in the dry, yellow earth of the north. Chinese food is one of the world's great cuisines and introduced spaghetti to Italy and tea to India.

This village is in north China near Datong. Bright yellow maize is drying in the sun.

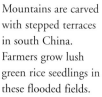

Mountains are carved with stepped terraces in south China. Farmers grow lush green rice seedlings in these flooded fields.

NEOLITHIC PERIOD

THE FIRST FARMERS lived in various parts of China 8000 years ago. They built homes in settled communities along the banks of China's main rivers. Each group had their own distinctive customs and styles for making objects. In the north, the Yangshao people lived along the banks of the Huang He (Yellow River) in over a thousand sites between 4500 and 2500 BC. They planted grain crops such as millet, wheat and barley. They made tools from wood, clay, stone and bone. They raised animals, including pigs, goats and dogs. They built houses with thatched roofs inside protected settlements. They fired and painted pottery. They also used lacquer (a tree sap) to protect and decorate objects. Some dressed in animal skins or spun cloth, including silk. They made jewellery from jade, shell and pottery. From about 2700 BC they practised acupuncture, which involves piercing the body with small needles to relieve pain. Archaeologists have found evidence of rice growing in Hunan dating back to about 6000 BC.

People living about 2500 BC along the banks of the Yellow River made these storage jars from coiled sausage-like strips of clay. They were baked in a fire pit and left to cool, then painted black and red.

Potters in Shandong or Shaanxi province about 2500–1700 BC invented a slow-turning wheel, which helped them to make pots with thin walls.

JADE CARVING

Neolithic peoples buried their dead with goods to prepare for an afterlife and built temples in which they offered gifts to gods. They worked jade into precious objects about 7000 years ago in Liaoning and Inner Mongolia. This very hard mineral was carved without metal tools. The earliest carved jades are luxury ornaments, tools or weapons used in ceremonies. The most important early jade-using people are the Hongshan (3800–2700 BC) in the northeast, around Liaoning province, and the Liangzhu (3000–2000 BC) in the southeast, centred on modern Shanghai. Hongshan people carved hoof-shaped hair ornaments, axes and pig-dragon pendants. Liangzhu people made discs with a hole in the middle, called bi, and tubes of jade, called cong. Ancient people buried these objects in the graves of the wealthy.

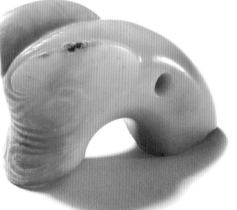

This jade carving, of a coiled dragon with the snout of a pig, was made by the Hongshan Neolithic people about 3500 BC.

This is one of the tallest cong jades, carved from a single jade boulder. Each corner has a mask with simple round eyes. It was made between 3000 and 2000 BC in Jiangsu or Zhejiang province.

XIA & SHANG DYNASTIES

T HE XIA DYNASTY (about 2000–1500 BC) marks the transition from the Neolithic to the Bronze Age. The Xia left no written records but archaeologists have discovered the remains of a palace and fortified city at Erlitou in Henan province. This is believed to be the site of their capital, dating from 1700 to 1500 BC. Bronze angular cups for heating wine were found there. A Shang king overthrew the Xia, and his own family then ruled for almost 500 years.

This bronze wine vessel supported by two rams was made in southern China about 1300–1100 BC, for banquets in the afterlife.

The Shang made human and animal sacrifices. Human skeletons have been found beneath the foundations of important buildings at Anyang. This bronze axe is decorated with a monster's face, with jagged teeth and fangs.

Shang metalworkers developed ways of using bronze to create weapons that were better than those of their enemies. The Shang believed in life after death. Alcohol, meats and cereals were offered to their dead relatives so that in return they would bring good fortune to the living. When an important man died, he was buried with weapons and a set of bronze containers so that he could continue to hold banquets after his death.

The Shang rulers were powerful and their society was highly organized. They built China's first cities. Their most impressive capital city was Anyang, which they established about 1300 BC.

The burial ground of the Shang kings at Anyang contained 11 royal graves and 1,000 other tombs. The king was buried with all the things that he might need as a king in the next world, including real animals and people. The last Shang king was defeated by the western state of Zhou in about 1050 BC.

EARLY WRITING

There is evidence of writing in China by 1200 BC. The Shang royal family kept written records. Shang kings believed their ancestors advised them through oracle bones. These were polished shoulder blades of oxen or the undershells of turtles. The back of the bone or shell was dug out in small roundels and hot rods were applied to the indents. This heat made 'T'-shaped cracks appear over the bone or shell. The patterns of cracks were then used to foretell the future. Scribes carved questions and answers into the bone or shell. A typical inscription might ask about the best time to grow crops, or whether the king would have success in battle. Writing has also been found on Shang bronzes, including the names of owners. These texts help us to understand Shang society.

This ox's shoulder blade has an inscription dateable to about 1200 BC. The text refers to sacrificing pigs and mentions the names of dead ancestors.

Other bronze-casting cultures in China at this time left no written records. The southern Shu people had contact with the Shang, but they had very different customs and rituals. This Shu bronze god or priest was made about 1200–1000 BC. It weighs 180 kg and measures 2.62 m high. It was excavated at Sanxingdui in Sichuan province.

9

WESTERN ZHOU DYNASTY

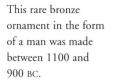

1050 TO 771 BC THE ZHOU GRADUALLY SPREAD EASTWARDS from their territory in northwest China, and in 1050 BC they defeated the Shang. Their rule lasted 800 years. They set up their first capital at Xi'an. The Zhou used the same written language as the Shang and shared the same rituals, including the worship of dead ancestors. They also used the same technology such as bronze casting to make weapons and vessels for use in rituals. At this time the idea developed that kings were sons of heaven, who were placed on the throne with a 'Mandate from Heaven'. So long as they continued to receive the blessings of Heaven, they could continue to rule. If they lost the goodwill of the gods, then another king would take over the Mandate and could rule in their place. After conquering the Shang, the Zhou king rewarded his relatives and supporters with presents of land, slaves and luxury goods.

This rare bronze ornament in the form of a man was made between 1100 and 900 BC.

The Western Zhou used bronze to decorate and protect their horses in battle. This bronze harness fitting is cast in the shape of a taotie, or monster mask, and was made between 1100 and 900 BC.

BRONZE CASTING

Bronze vessels that have survived into our time were buried either in tombs or in hoards. In 771 BC the Zhou were driven out of their capital and the Western Zhou dynasty ended. The wealthy then buried their sets of expensive bronze vessels in secret pits to protect them from their enemies. Bigger

vessels belonged to richer owners. Inscriptions on the ritual vessels show that people used them for feasts including different foods and wines. These meals were offered as gifts to the dead in the hope that in return they would act as go-betweens for the living with the spirits of the afterlife.

Bronzes were produced in very large numbers by using moulds. A clay model was first made and a mould was then constructed in pieces around it, like the thick peel of an orange. This outer mould was then peeled away in sections. It was later fitted back into shape with spacers to separate it from a clay core. Metalworkers poured hot liquid bronze (a mixture of copper and tin) into the space between the mould and the core. This would cool and harden so the mould and inner core could be removed, leaving a bronze vessel. The same furnace technology was also used in the ceramics industry. Mass production was achieved through the division of labour. Ancient bronze vessels today appear dull green or brown, but originally they would have sparkled like gold.

The inscription on this bronze food vessel records a gift to a man associated with the Duke of Kang, a brother of a Zhou king. It was made between 1100 and 1000 BC.

This is a detail of the inscription on the bronze food container above.

EASTERN ZHOU DYNASTY

770 TO 221 BC IN 771 BC, attacks by western nomads forced the Zhou to move their capital eastwards. The Eastern Zhou was a period of great inventions, including between 600 and 500 BC the world's first iron tools. These greatly changed farming, because heavy or waterlogged soil could now be ploughed and planted. The crossbow was invented between 400 and 300 BC. This powerful new weapon could fire a bolt with much greater force and reached further than an arrow from a bow.

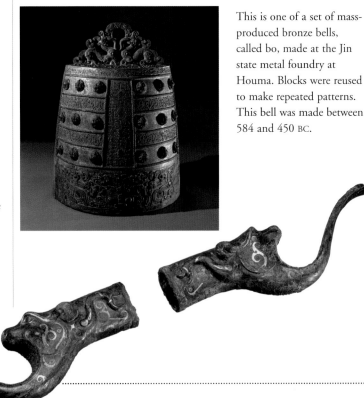

This is one of a set of mass-produced bronze bells, called bo, made at the Jin state metal foundry at Houma. Blocks were reused to make repeated patterns. This bell was made between 584 and 450 BC.

Belt hooks, weapon fittings, chariot parts and ritual vessels were decorated with gold, silver, malachite, jade or glass. These inlaid fittings are from a stand made for a crossbow between 399 and 221 BC.

PHILOSOPHY

Two great Chinese philosophers lived during a period when small states were battling one another within China. Confucius, Kong Fuzi (552–479 BC), was born in the state of Lu, in modern Shandong province. He was a scholar and travelled

between states explaining his ideas on government and social behaviour. For instance, he said a child should honour his parents, a servant should obey his master, and a gentleman should respect his king. If all people behaved well, there would be harmony. Confucius' sayings were written down by his followers in the Lun Yu (Analects). Although he was never thought to be a god, people built temples dedicated to Confucius.

Laozi (about 604–531 BC) is the legendary founder of Daoism. He is believed to have been born aged 70, with white hair. His philosophy was written down in the Dao Dejing (Way of the Dao) about 399–295 BC. Unlike Confucius, who suggested the best way to behave within society, Laozi advised withdrawing from society to live in harmony with nature. Daoism later developed into a religion with its own gods, temples and priests. Daoist ideas became mixed with popular beliefs and magic.

(Above left) A portrait of Confucius, one of China's greatest philosophers.

(Above right) Detail from a tile depicting Laozi, made at Jingdezhen between AD 1600 and 1640.

QIN DYNASTY

Between 230 and 221 BC, King Zheng of the Qin defeated six other states to unify the country. In 221 BC, he declared himself First Emperor. He built a magnificent palace, with a vast garden and hunting park, at his capital Xianyang.

The First Emperor created a Great Wall between the Chinese and the nomadic peoples of the north. At its longest, it measured 4,000 miles.

Although he only ruled for little more than a decade, his achievements are extraordinary. Before he came to power, each state had its own language, money and system for measuring weights and volumes. He forced people to use the same Qin weights, measures and axle widths for vehicles across the empire. He cut the number of written Chinese characters down to 3,000. He established a single currency. He joined together existing sections of wall to form a Great Wall of packed earth and built many important roads. He travelled all over China, announcing his achievements and having stone tablets set up on mountainsides. In many ways he was the founder of China.

The First Emperor was an authoritarian ruler. He imposed a strict set of laws based on a system of punishment and reward. He believed that people would only obey the law if they were afraid of being punished. Depending on the severity of the crime, punishments ranged

Nomads travelled about the north with their grazing animals. Periodically they made raids into China. This plaque showing a northern raider with a sword was made between 220 and 1 BC.

from cutting off ears, feet, hands or genitals to execution by slicing in half. Thousands of prisoners and soldiers were forced to work for the emperor: building his tomb, his capital, the Great Wall and the new roads which united the empire. It has been said that he collected books from all over China and burned those he didn't want people to read, but to this day we don't know if this story is true.

TERRACOTTA WARRIORS

Despite drinking many kinds of potions that he hoped would help him to live longer, he died in 210 BC and was buried in an underground palace specially built for him. The First Emperor's tomb has not yet been excavated, but in 100 BC Sima Qian described it. Nearly 7,000 larger than life size terracotta warriors were buried in battle formation to the east of his tomb. These clay soldiers, cavalrymen and generals replaced real people. They were equipped with real weapons including crossbows and spears. Originally the warriors were all colourfully painted to look life-like. They were mass-produced and, although the faces look distinctive, they are made up of a selection of nose, eye and mouth types. The potters assembled the faces like a policeman guessing the appearance of a criminal. Archaeologists continue to excavate at the site. Recent discoveries include storage pits packed with sets of stone armour and an underground waterway filled with exotic birds made from bronze.

This is one of the terracotta army soldiers who guarded the tomb of the First Emperor.

This bronze horse-drawn chariot model was made for the First Emperor, so he could make inspection tours of his extensive empire in the afterlife.

HAN DYNASTY &
THE PERIOD OF DISUNITY

Buddhism was introduced to China from India in the 1st century AD. This gilt-bronze Bodhisattva is dated AD 471.

206 BC TO AD 589 L IU BANG, A GOVERNMENT OFFICIAL, founded the Han dynasty with its capital at Chang'an. At its height, the Han empire extended from Korea in the east to Xinjiang in the north and Vietnam in the south. It was one of the 'Golden Ages' of Chinese history. Han emperors encouraged trade and foreign contact. The trade routes that crossed the deserts between China and the Middle East were known collectively as the Silk Road. Under Emperor Wudi (140–87 BC), these routes brought new ideas to China, including Buddhism in the 1st century AD, and sent silk, spices and other luxury goods abroad.

BUREAUCRACY

The Han emperors replaced nobles with officials who had passed Confucian public examinations. These civil servants collected government taxes and kept law and order. Officials ran state factories making bronzes, lacquer and textile goods. Salt and coal were mined and controlled by state monopolies. An official named Cai Lun invented a new way to make paper in 105 BC, which replaced hemp paper, silk, bamboo strip books, wood and stone tablets for keeping records.

This lavish bronze lamp is inlaid with silver and gold. It was made between 206 and 1 BC and could have been among the treasures in a tomb.

TOMBS

In the Han dynasty, people believed they had two souls: the hun, which became immortal, and the po, which lived on in an underworld. Real objects were replaced by ceramic replicas in tombs. Servants were no longer buried with their masters but were substituted by clay models of servants. Relatives buried pottery model buildings, animals and even money trees to ensure eternal wealth. Tombs were built of brick, and the walls were painted or stamped with religious images and scenes of everyday life. Jade was believed to preserve the corpse. In wealthy burials, jade plaques were placed on the eyes, jade plugs put up the nose and a cicada-shaped jade sealed the mouth. Some Han princes were buried in whole suits made of jade plaques stitched together.

The Han dynasty collapsed through a combination of weak emperors and natural disasters. A period of division followed, when foreign tribes took control of the north while people in the south continued to pursue Han traditions.

These two tomb figures were made between AD 25 and 220. They are engaged in a lively game of Liu Bo, a kind of backgammon played with counters.

This detail shows a brave lady saving the emperor from a wild bear. It is part of a scene from a long handscroll painting illustrating the Nushi zhen (Admonitions of the Instructress to the Court Ladies), painted during the Tang dynasty (AD 618–906) in the style of Gu Kaizhi (AD 344–405).

17

SUI & TANG DYNASTIES

THE PERIOD OF DISUNITY ENDED in AD 589 when the first Sui emperor reunified China. The Sui dynasty (AD 589–618) lasted less than thirty years, but they built the 1,500-km long Grand Canal, encouraged the spread of Buddhism and paved the way for the Tang dynasty, another of China's 'Golden Ages'.

TANG DYNASTY

Under the Tang emperors (AD 618–906), China became the most powerful empire in the world. In the 7th century AD, over a million people lived in the capital city, Chang'an – then the world's biggest city. By the 8th century, China was a superpower and the world's richest nation. But in AD 906 peasants revolted, overthrowing the last Tang emperor.

The Grand Canal linked the Huang He and Chang Jiang rivers and joined existing canals. People paid tax to the government in grain and the Grand Canal ensured its safe transportation to the capital. As the population grew, imported rice from the south was vital to feed the greater number of people.

This photograph shows a camel train outside Beijing in the 1920s or 1930s.

BUDDHISM, TRADE AND THE SILK ROAD

During the Tang dynasty, foreigners settled in Chinese cities and brought with them their languages, religions and customs. Nestorian Christians and followers of Islam were tolerated. Foreign ambassadors visited the court. By ship and by camel train, merchants brought exotic foreign luxury goods to China, including silver, gold and glass tablewares as well as new spices and foods such as grapes and walnuts. They also brought new entertainments and fashions. Inspired by visiting Persians, Emperor Xuanzong (AD 685–762) took part in international polo matches in his pleasure gardens.

Chinese people adopted foreign ideas, too. A Chinese pilgrim monk, Xuan Zang (AD 602–64), travelled to India and brought back Buddhist scriptures written in Sanskrit which scholars then translated into Chinese. Chinese craftsmen adopted Indian styles for carving sculpture. Potters made glazed ceramic imitations of foreign luxury goods for the tombs of wealthy people. Painters decorating a Buddhist cave site near the Silk Road oasis town of Dunhuang were inspired by Chinese, Tibetan and Central Asian styles.

Chinese potters invented porcelain in about AD 600 and merchants shipped ceramics abroad to India, the Middle East and Africa. China's textile industries prospered and fine silks were also exported.

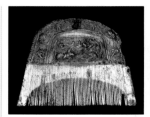

Chinese women wore very tall, elaborate hairstyles that were held in place by jade, gold, silver, glass and ivory pins and combs. Under foreign influence, gold and silver became highly prized during the Tang dynasty.

This detail of a Buddhist painting from Dunhuang shows the voluptuous Tang lady who paid for the painting wearing fine silk clothes and expensive hair ornaments. It was painted between AD 851 and 900.

This modern ink on paper hanging scroll painting of the poet Du Fu was painted by Hua Junwu between 1951 and 1996.

(Above right) This colour print shows the poet Li Bo writing a hundred verses while drinking wine and seated on a veranda. His consumption of alcohol was legendary.

POETRY

Learning to write poetry was an important part of education during the Tang dynasty and some of the finest poetry was written in classical Chinese. The work of at least 10,000 poets survives today. The most famous of these poets are Li Bo (AD 701–62) and Du Fu (AD 712–70). Li Bo withdrew from court life and his poetry is full of Daoist imagery. He was also a famous drunkard and drowned while trying to embrace the reflection of the moon in the water. By contrast, Du Fu is celebrated as a poet of Chinese history and military tactics. Woodblock printing was invented and used on mass-produced paper in the Tang dynasty. Before this, every book had to be copied out by hand. Printing resulted in an increase in the number of books in circulation and more people learned to read.

CALLIGRAPHY

Calligraphy is considered the highest art form in China. Chinese characters must be drawn with perfect balance and proportion, and the order in which the strokes are made always follows a set pattern. The ideal amount of ink must be ground from an ink cake and mixed with a little water on an ink stone. The animal-hair brush has to be loaded with the right amount of ink. Too much ink and the calligraphy will run, too little and the dry brush will scratch the paper. Seal script, used by the First Emperor, is still used for seals today as a personal signature. Clerical script, developed about 200 BC, was used for record keeping. An easy-to-read script was later used for ordinary writing and printed books. Grass script was more suitable for fast writing, such as taking notes.

These items are used for writing: brush washer, brush stand, brush, red seal paste in a round box, seal, ink stone and ink cake.

This modern hanging scroll painting of an old calligrapher was painted by Huang Yongyu. Traditional Chinese writing reads from the top down and from right to left, starting in the top right corner. Modern Chinese writing usually reads across from left to right, starting in the top left corner.

21

FIVE DYNASTIES, LIAO, JIN & SONG DYNASTIES

AD 907 TO 1279 AFTER THE COLLAPSE OF THE TANG DYNASTY in AD 906, China was again divided into warring kingdoms. In the northeast, the semi-nomadic Qidan (Khitan) people ruled as the Liao dynasty (AD 907–1125), with their capital in Beijing. The rest of the north was divided into five separate kingdoms called the Five Dynasties, while the south was divided into Ten Kingdoms.

SONG DYNASTY

In AD 960, an army general named Zhao Kuangyin united China and founded the Song dynasty. Farmers grew a new type of rice that yielded two or three crops a year, so a larger population could be fed and cities grew rapidly. The Northern Song (AD 960–1126) had their capital at the northern city of Kaifeng and controlled both northern and southern China. In AD 1127, the Song were defeated by the invading Jurchens, who had established the Jin dynasty (AD 1115–1234) in the north, and had to move their capital from Kaifeng to the southern city of Hangzhou.

When the Song lost control of the north of China they also lost control of the Silk Road and had to turn to the sea for trade. They built huge ships with

This polychrome wooden figure of a Bodhisattva was made in the Jin dynasty (AD 1115–1234).

This porcelain wine ewer and warming basin were made between AD 1126 and 1279 at Jingdezhen.

watertight hulls and stern-post rudders for steering. They used compasses and travelled as far as India and the Persian Gulf.

ARTS AND CRAFTS

Vast numbers of ceramics were produced all over the country.

Collectors especially admired those with green to blue glazes. Chinese connoisseurs also distinguished between the decorative styles of professional court painters and the more restrained monochrome ink paintings of amateur scholars. Landscape painting was the most highly regarded. Fine silks were woven in the Hangzhou region. Metalworkers made copies of ancient bronzes, but they were more elongated and had simpler decoration than the originals.

This detail is from a scroll painting once said to be by Zhao Ji, the emperor Huizong (AD 1110–26).

This detail is from 'Going up River on the Qingming Festival', a copy made between 1500 and 1644 of a painting by Zhang Zeduan of Kaifeng (AD 1085–1145).

23

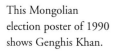

This Mongolian election poster of 1990 shows Genghis Khan.

This Mongolian farmer is milking a mare in the 1920s or 1930s. Drinking fermented mare's milk is a Mongolian custom.

YUAN DYNASTY

AD 1279 TO 1368

Genghis Khan (about AD 1167–1227) united the northern peoples living in the Mongolian grasslands and founded the Mongol empire. At its height, this stretched from East Asia to Europe. Genghis Khan's grandson, Khubilai Khan (AD 1260–94), invaded China for its natural resources and vast supplies of labour. He established a lavish new winter capital in what is now Beijing and declared himself emperor. Although the Mongols were essentially nomads (travellers), they quickly adopted Chinese habits and customs including the Chinese system of bureaucracy.

THE MONGOLS

The Mongols were suspicious of the Han Chinese scholars they had conquered and appointed Mongol, Tibetan or other non-Chinese officials to the main government posts. This resulted in a greater cultural mix at court. Some first-hand descriptions of travels to China were written in European languages at this time, including Marco Polo's account of 1299. Sea and overland trade were encouraged across the vast Mongolian empire. Renovation of the Grand Canal and the rebuilding of roads improved transport for commerce. Trade between East and West flourished, and Middle Eastern merchants traded directly with China. The Mongols embraced different cultures, and this attitude encouraged religious understanding. Muslims from Central

Asia converted many people in northwest and southwest China to Islam. Muslims brought with them skills in astronomy and map-making. Christianity and Tibetan Buddhism were also tolerated.

Despite this being a period of foreign rule, Chinese culture flourished and was enriched by foreign influences. Some of the finest Chinese paintings were made by scholar-artists such as Ni Zan (1301–74), who retired from court life to paint sparse landscapes with ink and brush. Drama and the novel both developed through the use of a written language which was now much closer to spoken Chinese. Natural disasters, peasant uprisings, infighting among the Mongols and a decline in their military power eventually led to the collapse of the Yuan dynasty in 1368.

This detail of 'The Fascination of Nature', a handscroll painting by Xie Chufang dated 1321, shows beautifully painted insects and plants.

Instead of single glaze colours, the Mongols preferred bold painted designs. Blue and white wares were made for temple and everyday use in China and were also traded to the Middle East and Southeast Asia. This covered wine jar is decorated with a dragon.

MING DYNASTY

ZHU YUANZHANG (1328–98) was a rebel leader who conquered the Mongols and founded the Ming dynasty. He built his capital at Nanjing and his descendants ruled China for three centuries. Technology advanced, cities expanded and more people than ever learned to read and write. The Great Wall and Grand Canal were restored.

FORBIDDEN CITY

In 1403 Zhu Yuanzhang was succeeded by his son, who moved the capital to Beijing where, between 1406 and 1421, he built the Forbidden City. This remains the best-preserved monument to China's traditional architecture, with its red timber frame and yellow-glazed roof tiles. It is also the largest complex of intact historic buildings in the world, with some 800 buildings containing 9,000 rooms. It was called the 'Forbidden City' because common people were forbidden to enter without special permission. It was the centre of government administration and also the private residence of the 24 emperors of the Ming and Qing dynasties. In 1925 it

This detail of an ancestral portrait of the Ming emperor Zhengde shows him dressed in imperial yellow dragon robes. Such pictures were not intended to be seen by anyone outside the imperial family.

The Forbidden City.

became the Palace Museum and now houses some of China's most important art treasures and paintings.

Between 1405 and 1433 the Muslim admiral Zheng He set out on seven grand seafaring expeditions to Southeast Asia, India, the Middle East and East Africa. His well-armed fleet was the largest in the world at the time. The emperor equipped him with lavish gifts for foreign kings. Between 1417 and 1419 he returned to China with a giraffe from Africa for the imperial zoo.

Although some individual Europeans had earlier travelled to China, contact was still limited. Europeans wanted to develop direct trade with China, and in 1557 Portuguese merchants established a base at Aomen (Macao). The Roman Catholic church also wished to expand its influence, and Jesuit priests such as the Italian Matteo Ricci (1552–1609) went to China as missionaries.

This blue and white porcelain pilgrim flask was made between 1403 and 1424. Its shape is typical of the Middle East, showing the impact of the region on Ming court taste.

This shrine, made in 1406, shows Daoist, Buddhist and popular gods. In the top niche is Zhenwu, a popular military deity.

QING DYNASTY

By THE END OF THE MING DYNASTY, government treasuries had been depleted by years of military campaigns, extravagance and corruption. Peasants revolted against high taxes. Rebel armies invaded the Forbidden City. A Manchu clan from the grasslands of the northeast then founded the Qing dynasty.

This 17th-century gilt-silver crown has many attached decorations, including flowers, flaming pearls, dragons and phoenix.

MANCHU RULE

China was governed by three great emperors in the 18th century: Kangxi (1662–1722), Yongzheng (1723–35) and Qianlong (1736–95). Qing emperors absorbed native Chinese culture and reinstated the imperial examination system. Direct trade with Europe was encouraged and European merchants set up offices in Guangzhou (Canton)

From 1715 the Chinese government made Guangzhou the only open port for official trade with Europeans. This punchbowl, made between AD 1780 and 1790, shows foreign factories built along the banks of the Pearl River at Guangzhou. Each flies its national flag.

to export porcelain, tea and silk. In 1792, Lord George Macartney (1737–1806) led the first embassy from Britain to China, although he failed to improve Chinese–British trade.

The 19th century was overshadowed by conflicts. The First Opium War (1839–42) between Britain and China began as an attempt to stop the English East India Company trading the addictive drug opium in exchange for Chinese tea, silk and porcelain. China's outdated military equipment and poor strategy were no match for British forces. In 1856 the Second Opium War broke out, and French and English troops occupied Beijing, first looting and then burning down the Summer Palace.

The Taiping Rebellion (1851–64) was a terrible civil war costing at least 20 million civilian and army lives. The Empress Dowager Cixi controlled China from behind the scenes for 47 years. She was a concubine of the emperor Xianfeng (1850–61), mother of the emperor Tongzhi (1862–74) and aunt of the emperor Guangxu (1875–1908). In 1894–5 China waged war with Japan. In 1900, there was a violent uprising against foreigners, called the Boxer Rebellion. In 1908, Puyi (1906–67), then aged two, succeeded to the throne. On 12 February 1912, the last emperor – then a five-year-old child – was forced to abdicate, and a republic was established.

Peking (Beijing) opera was extremely popular at the Qing dynasty court from the mid 19th century. The traditional repertoire includes more than 1,000 works. This modern coloured papercut shows one of the male roles.

LATER HISTORY

Sun Yat Sen (1866–1925) became the first head of the Nationalist government in 1911. In 1912, Yuan Shikai (1859–1916) became President of the Republic of China. He ruled as a dictator and four years later declared himself emperor. After his death there was no single leader, and warlords controlled the army. In 1921 the Chinese Communist Party was founded in Shanghai out of this chaos. From 1928 the Nationalist Party ruled China from Nanjing, led by Chiang Kai-shek (1887–1975).

This detail from a poster shows Mao Zedong on the Long March.

In 1934 the Communists were forced to retreat. In the Long March, 100,000 people walked nearly 6,000 miles across China, from Jiangxi in the southeast to Yan'an in the northwest. Only a fifth of them survived. During this epic year-long journey, Mao Zedong (1893–1976) emerged as leader. Japan was defeated in the Second World War in 1945, but civil war continued in China until the Communists defeated the Nationalists. Chiang Kai-shek and his followers fled to the island of Taiwan, which became the Republic of China. On 1 October 1949, the People's Republic of China was founded in mainland China with Chairman Mao as its leader. Between 1966 and 1976 Mao led a Cultural Revolution, supported by a young militia